PROBLEM SOLVING EXPERIENCES

MAKING SENSE OF MATHEMATICS

Grade 6

Randall I. Charles
Frank K. Lester
Diana V. Lambdin

Richard Caulfield
Christine Oster
Julie A. Sliva

DALE SEYMOUR PUBLICATIONS

Pearson Learning Group

The following people contributed to the development of this product:

Art and Design: John Maddalone, Judith Mates, Elizabeth Nemeth, Jim O'Shea

Editorial: Danielle Camaleri, Linda Dorf, Constance Shrier

Inventory: Joy Rudy

Marketing: Douglas Falk, Clare Harrison

Production: Lorraine Allen, Irene Belinsky, Carlos Blas, Mark Cirillo, Karen Edmonds, Jeffrey Engel, Leslie Greenberg, Josh Hammond, Nathan Kinney, Suellen Leavy, Alia Lesser, Susan Levine, Jennifer McCormack, Cathy Pawlowski, Cindy Talocci

Publishing Operations: Travis Bailey, Richetta Lobban, Debi Schlott

ISBN 0-7690-3247-8

Printed in the United States of America

1 2 3 4 5 6 7 8 9   08 07 06 05 04

Dale Seymour Publications

Pearson Learning Group

1-800-321-3106
www.pearsonlearning.com

Contents

A Note From the Authors

Math problems are all around, not just in books! Have you ever figured out how much more money you need to buy something special, or how long it will take to drive somewhere? Those are math problems, too, the kind that come up all the time.

One thing is for sure: With so many math problems about, it helps to be a good math problem solver! This book will help you reach that goal. You'll learn that there are many ways to solve problems. You'll also learn that most problems can be solved in more than one way.

At first, you might be a bit worried about solving math problems. That's okay. Chances are good that other students feel the same way. Solving problems isn't always easy, but practice will help you get better at it.

Remember: Always write your answer in a complete sentence. That will help you answer the problem correctly.

Problem-Solving Plan

Read and Understand

⭐ **Think about what you know.**
- Tell the problem in your own words.
- Identify key facts and details.

⭐ **Think about what you're trying to find.**
- Tell what the question is asking.
- Show the main idea.

Plan and Solve

⭐ **Choose a strategy.**
- Think about a strategy or strategies that may help you solve the problem.

⭐ **Stuck? Don't give up. Try these:**
- Reread the problem.
- Tell the problem in your own words.
- Tell what you know.
- Identify key facts and details.
- Show the main idea.
- Try a different strategy.
- Retrace your steps.

⭐ **Answer the question in the problem.**

Look Back and Check

⭐ **Check your answer.**
- Did you answer the right question?
- Use estimation and reasoning to decide if the answer makes sense.

⭐ **Check your work.**
- Compare your work to the information in the problem.
- Check to be sure you used the correct operation or method.

List of Problem-Solving Strategies

Some of the problems in this book can be solved using one of the strategies shown in the table below. The table shows the strategies we think make sense for particular problems.

There are usually many ways to solve a problem, however. If you can think of another way to solve any of the problems listed, that's great! Share your way with your teacher and classmates.

Problem-Solving Strategies	Problems
Use Objects	1, 71
Draw a Picture	6, 86
Look for a Pattern	11, 81
Make a Table	16, 136, 146
Try, Check, and Revise	46, 116
Make an Organized List	36, 106
Make a Graph	51, 121
Use Logical Reasoning	41, 111
Write an Equation	26, 61, 96, 131, 141
Work Backward	21, 56, 91, 126
Make a Simpler Problem	31, 66, 76, 101

1 The Ringtoss Game

Solve. Use objects.

Sam made a ringtoss game for the school carnival. He used 4 pegs and placed them in a straight line. The green peg is 8 inches to the right of the red peg. The yellow peg is 24 inches to the left of the green peg. The blue peg is halfway between the yellow peg and the red peg. What is the distance between the blue peg and the green peg?

> You can **USE OBJECTS** to solve this problem because
>
> • The numbers in the problem are small
>
> • There is something in the problem that you can show with objects
>
> How to **USE OBJECTS**
>
> **Step 1:** Choose objects to act out the problem.
>
> **Step 2:** Use the objects to show the given information.
>
> **Step 3:** Act out the problem.
>
> **Step 4:** Find the answer in your work.

Answer _____

Convince Me Explain how you solved the problem.

Math Journal Why is using objects a useful strategy for solving the problem?

2) Sprucing Things Up

Estimate. Use rounding.
Circle the letter of the correct answer.

Arifa bought some new furniture for her apartment. She bought a couch for $789, a kitchen table for $210, and a bed for $612. About how much did Arifa spend altogether?

A. about $2,100

B. about $160

C. about $1,600

D. about $1,400

3) What's the Rule?

Here are 3 cube buildings in a pattern.
Use cubes or draw to show the next 2 buildings.
Complete the next 2 columns in the table.
Then record the number of cubes in a building with a 10-cube tower and in a building with a 100-cube tower. Write the rule for the number of cubes in any building in this pattern.

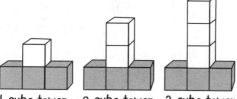

1-cube tower 4 total cubes 2-cube tower 5 total cubes 3-cube tower 6 total cubes

Number of Cubes in Tower	1	2	3	4	5	10	100
Total Number of Cubes in Building	4	5	6				

Rule _____

Math Journal What does the building look like when there are 10 total cubes?

4) Plant Diet

Solve.

Marcia is doing a science experiment with 24 plants. She gives each plant 3 ounces (oz) of a special growth liquid twice a week. How many quarts of the growth liquid does she give all the plants in 1 week? *(Hint: 1 quart = 32 oz)*

Hidden Question 1 How much growth liquid does 1 plant get in 1 week?

Answer _____

Hidden Question 2 How many ounces of growth liquid does Marcia give all the plants in 1 week?

Answer _____

Final Question How many quarts of growth liquid does Marcia give all the plants in 1 week?

Answer _____

5) Out to Pasture

Solve. Explain your work.

Larry has 36 sections of wooden fencing. Each section is 6 feet long. He plans to use all the sections to surround a rectangular pasture. What is the area of the largest pasture he could create?

Answer _____

Math Journal How many different-size rectangular pastures could Larry make? List the different sizes of each pasture.

6 Marching On

Solve. Draw a picture.

A marching band practiced a march on the school football field. It took the band 1 minute to march forward 10 meters (m). Then it marched backward 5 m. That took 1 minute also. The band continued to march forward and backward. The band completed the march when it had moved forward 35 m from its starting point. How long did it take the band to complete the march?

> You can **DRAW A PICTURE** to solve this problem because
>
> • It is easy to draw a picture to show the given information
>
> • A picture can help you visualize the problem
>
> How to **DRAW A PICTURE**
>
> **Step 1:** Draw a simple picture to show part of the given information.
>
> **Step 2:** Complete the picture.
>
> **Step 3:** Use the picture to solve the problem.

Answer _____

Convince Me Explain how you solved the problem

Math Journal How many meters forward had the band marched from its starting point after 4 minutes? Explain.

7) For a Good Cause

Estimate. Use compatible numbers.
Circle the letter of the correct answer.

A charity has raised money over the past four months. The table shows how much money the charity collected each month. About how much did the charity collect altogether?

A. about $210

B. about $350

C. about $110

D. about $335

| Money Collected for Charity ||
Month	Amount Collected
January	$68.35
February	$45.05
March	$12.10
April	$87.24

⭐ **THINK**

Using compatible numbers is one way to estimate. Replace numbers with numbers that are close and easy to use in your head.

Example
346 + 192
Replace 346 with $\quad$ 345
Replace 192 with $\quad \underline{+\ 190}$
$\qquad\qquad\qquad$ 535

346 + 192 is about 535.

---

8) What's the Bench Rule?

Here are three benches in a pattern.
Draw the next 2 benches.
Complete the next 2 columns in the table.
Then record the number of seats for the bench with 10 legs and for the bench with 100 legs.
Write the rule that you can use to tell the number of seats for any bench in this pattern.

2 legs, 1 seat

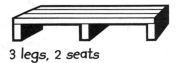
3 legs, 2 seats

4 legs, 3 seats

Number of Legs	2	3	4	5	6	10	100
Total Number of Seats	1	2	3				

Rule _____

Math Journal What does the bench look like when there are 20 legs?

⑨ Around the Water Cooler

THINK

To solve multiple-step problems, you need to

1. Answer the Hidden Question(s)

2. Use your answer(s) to the Hidden Question(s) to answer the Final Question

Solve.

A large office building uses 120 5-gallon bottles of spring water in one month. A crate of 8 bottles of water costs $18.50. How much does the office building spend on bottled water in a month?

Hidden Question How many crates of bottled water does the office use in one month?

Answer _____

_____

TEST TIP

Is your answer reasonable? Estimate to check.

Final Question How much does the office spend on bottled water in a month?

Answer _____

_____

⑩ Patrick's Patches

Solve. Explain your work.

The floor in Patrick's new apartment has a patch with a 10-ft perimeter where 5 tiles are missing and at least one side of a tile matches a side on another tile. The landlord gave Patrick 5 new square tiles to cover the patch. Each tile is 1 ft by 1 ft. What is the shape of the area that needs to be covered?

Answer _____

Math Journal How many different ways can 5 tiles be organized so that each side of a tile matches with at least one side from another tile? Draw each arrangement.

(11) Doing Push-ups

Solve. Look for a pattern.

Martin is following an exercise program. He plans to do 1 push-up the first day, 4 push-ups the second day, 7 push-ups the third day, 10 push-ups the fourth day, and so on, until he reaches his goal of at least 30 push-ups each day. How many days must Martin exercise to reach his goal of 30 push-ups each day?

You can **LOOK FOR A PATTERN** to solve this problem because

- Something repeats or changes

- What repeats or changes does so in the same way every time

How to **LOOK FOR A PATTERN**

Step 1: Look for what repeats or changes.

Step 2: Check that what repeats or changes does so in the same way every time.

Step 3: Describe the pattern.

Step 4: Use the pattern to find the answer.

Answer _____

Convince Me Explain how you solved the problem.

Math Journal Describe the number pattern in the problem. Then write a similar number pattern using at least six numbers and describe it.

(12) Summertime Savings

Summer	2000	2001	2002	2003
Amount Saved	$98	$134	$546	$785

Estimate. Use front-end estimation.
Circle the letter of the correct answer.

Manuel worked for four summers to save money for college. The chart shows how much money he saved each summer. About how much money did Manuel save for college altogether?

- **A.** about $240
- **B.** about $1,400
- **C.** about $1,300
- **D.** about $1,600

⭐ **THINK**

Using front-end digits is one way to estimate. Add, subtract, multiply, or divide the front-end digits. Then, adjust the estimate by looking at the digits to the right.

Example

193 + 136 is about 100 + 100 = 200.

93 + 36 is about 90 + 40 = 130.

200 + 130 = 330, so 193 + 136 is about 330.

---

(13) What's the Party Table Rule?

Here are 3 party tables in a pattern.
Draw the next 2 sets of party tables in the pattern.
Complete the next 2 columns in the table.
Then record the number of guests that can be seated at 10 tables and at 100 tables.
Write the rule that you can use to tell the number of guests for any group of party tables in this pattern.

1 table, 4 guests

2 tables, 8 guests

3 tables, 12 guests

Number of Party Tables	1	2	3	4	5	10	100
Number of Guests	4	8	12				

Rule _____

Math Journal How many party tables are needed to seat 48 guests?

⭐ **THINK**

The rule for this pattern is a mathematical sentence that tells how to find the number of guests when you know the number of party tables.

(14) A Mountain of a Bargain!

Solve.

Maxwell's Ski Shop is having a sale. Caitlin wants to buy all the equipment separately. Karen tells Caitlin it will cost less to buy the equipment as a package. Does it cost less to buy the pieces separately or as a package? How much less?

Hidden Question How much does it cost to buy the items separately?

Answer _____

_____

★ THINK

To solve multiple-step problems, you need to

1. Answer the Hidden Question(s)

2. Use your answer(s) to the Hidden Question(s) to answer the Final Question

Final Question Does it cost less to buy the pieces separately or as a package? How much less?

Answer _____

(15) That's Sum Wheel!

Solve. Explain your work.

The picture shows the prize wheel at the school carnival. A player spins the wheel 3 times to win a prize. A different prize is given for each possible three-number sum. How many different prizes are there?

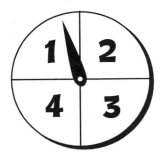

TEST TIP

Think about which problem-solving strategies might help you.

Answer _____

Math Journal What is the lowest possible sum you can get with 3 spins? What is the highest possible sum you can get with 3 spins? Explain.

16 A Hair Story

Solve. Make a Table.

In Colorville, about 15 out of every 50 people are blond. The town has a population of about 500. About how many people in Colorville are blond?

You can **MAKE A TABLE** to solve this problem because

- It has two or more quantities that are related

- Each quantity changes in a pattern

How to **MAKE A TABLE**

Step 1: Set up the table with the correct columns, rows, and labels.

Step 2: Enter the data you know into the table.

Step 3: Look for a pattern. Extend the pattern.

Step 4: Find the answer in the table.

Answer _____

Convince Me Explain how you solved the problem.

Math Journal Describe the number patterns in the table.

(17) Cold Months, High Bills

Estimate. Use clustering.
Circle the letter of the correct answer.

During the winter, Daniel's gas bills are high because he turns on the heat. In December his bill was $78.43. His January bill was $80.56. In February his bill was $82.13, and in March his bill was $76.48. About how much were Daniel's gas bills altogether?

A. about $240

B. about $260

C. about $320

D. about $400

Math Journal Explain why you chose the compatible number you used to estimate.

(18) What's the Mouse House Rule?

Here are 3 mouse houses in a pattern.
Use cubes or draw to show the next 2 houses.
Complete the next 2 columns in the table.
Then record the number of cubes for the house with 10 mice and the house with 100 mice.
Write the rule for the number of cubes for any number of mice in this pattern.

1 mouse, 5 cubes

2 mice, 8 cubes

3 mice, 11 cubes

Number of Mice in House	1	2	3	4	5	10	100
Total Number of Cubes for House	5	8	11				

Rule _____

19 Average Bowlers

Solve.

The bowler with the highest average score after three games is the winner. Who finished first? Second? Third?

	Taj	Sing	Kia
Game 1	135	152	181
Game 2	145	157	123
Game 3	175	161	131

Hidden Question What is each player's average score?

Answer _____

_____

_____

★ THINK

To solve multiple-step problems, you need to

1. Answer the Hidden Question(s)

2. Use your answer(s) to the Hidden Question(s) to answer the Final Question

Final Question Who finished first? Second? Third?

Answer _____

Math Journal How did you find each player's average score?

20 Next Rest

Solve. Explain your work.

A group of students hiked through the mountains. There were rest areas every 1.3 miles. The group rested only after they had traveled a distance that is a whole number of miles. The rest areas are numbered consecutively.

1. At what number rest area did the group stop first? How many miles had they traveled at that point?

2. At what number rest area did the group stop second?

Answer _____

_____

(21) Fish Tale

Solve. Work backward.

Timmy, John, George, and Ricardo went fishing. Each boy caught 1 fish. Timmy's fish was twice as long as John's fish. John's fish was 9 centimeters (cm) shorter than George's fish. George's fish was 12 cm longer than Ricardo's fish. Ricardo's fish was 18 cm long. How long was Timmy's fish?

You can **WORK BACKWARD** to solve this problem because

- An end amount and some information about each unknown amount are given

- Each unknown amount can be found by comparing it to the end amount or to other amounts

How to **WORK BACKWARD**

Step 1: Identify what is unknown.

Step 2: Draw a picture or describe how each amount compares to other amounts, starting with what is unknown at the beginning.

Step 3: Work backward from the end, using the given information.

Answer _____

Convince Me Explain how you solved the problem.

Math Journal How can you check your answer?

22 Jelly Jars

Estimate. Use rounding.
Circle the letter of the correct answer.

Ann makes 33 jars of jelly each week. About how many jars of jelly does she make in a year?

A. about 20 jars

B. about 80 jars

C. about 300 jars

D. about 1,500 jars

★**THINK**

Rounding numbers to the nearest 10, 100, or 1,000 is one way to estimate.

Example
136×12

$$\begin{array}{rll} 136 & \text{rounds to} & 140 \\ \times\ 12 & \text{rounds to} & \times\ 10 \\ \hline & & 1,400 \end{array}$$

136×12 is about 1,400.

23 What's the Building Rule?

Here are 3 buildings in a pattern.
Use cubes or draw to show the next 2 buildings.
Complete the next 2 columns in the table.
Then record the number of cubes in building 10 and building 100. Write the rule for the number of cubes for any building in this pattern.

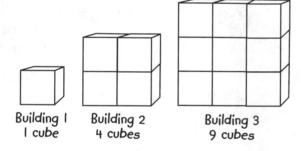

Building 1
1 cube

Building 2
4 cubes

Building 3
9 cubes

Building Number	1	2	3	4	5	10	100
Cubes in Building	1	4	9				

Rule _____

Math Journal What does the building with 64 cubes look like?

★**THINK**

The rule for this pattern is a mathematical sentence that tells how to find the number of cubes in the building when you know the building number.

TEST TIP

Check if your answer is clear and easy to follow.

(24) Row by Row

Solve.

In the York Theater, rows 15 through 33 are reserved for groups. There are 25 seats in each row. How many reserved seats are there altogether?

Hidden Question How many rows are in the reserved section?

Answer _____

_____

Final Question How many reserved seats are there altogether?

Answer _____

(25) Perfect Squares

Solve. Explain your work.

What two perfect squares have a sum of 52? *(Hint: A perfect square is the product of a whole number multiplied by itself.)*

Answer _____

Math Journal What two perfect squares have a product of 225? Explain how you found your answer.

26 Summer Fun

Solve. Write an equation.

Ling and her sister spend three days a week in the summertime at the Belmont Street Swimming Pool. The pool is rectangular. It is 12 times longer than it is wide. The perimeter of the pool is 910 feet. How wide is the pool?

You can **WRITE AN EQUATION** to solve this problem because

- You need to find a quantity that is unknown

- There is a relationship between the unknown quantity and other quantities that involves a mathematical operation

How to **WRITE AN EQUATION**

Step 1: Show the main idea of the problem.

Step 2: Decide which operation goes with the main idea.

Step 3: Use a letter to show what you are trying to find.

Step 4: Write and solve the equation.

Answer _____

Convince Me Explain how you solved the problem.

Math Journal What is the unknown quantity in the problem?

27 Get Registered!

Estimate. Use compatible numbers.
Circle the letter of the correct answer.

Day	Day 1	Day 2	Day 3	Day 4	Day 5
Voters Registered	1,736	2,111	1,929	2,034	2,323

Bainbridge had a voter registration drive. The table shows the number of people who registered to vote in five days. About how many people registered to vote during those five days?

A. about 101,000 people

B. about 10,000 people

C. about 6,000 people

D. about 15,000 people

★THINK

Using compatible numbers is one way to estimate. Replace numbers with numbers that are close and easy to use in your head.

Example
119 × 23
Replace 119 with   100
Replace 23 with   × 25
                      ‾‾‾‾‾‾‾
                      2,500
119 × 23 is about 2,500.

28 Family Pets

Solve.

The scatter plot tells about pets in four families. Use the clues to decide which point on the plot shows each family. Label each point with the first letter of the family's name.

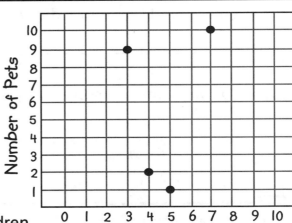

Clues
• The Benitez family has two adults and two children. Each child has a cat.
• There are 7 people in the Applewood family. Two people have one dog each, and Sandy has 8 fish!
• In the Dennis family, each person has 3 hamsters!
• The Chase family has 5 people but only one pet.

★THINK

What number pair does each point represent?

Math Journal How many people are in the Dennis family? Explain how you know.

(29) Pricey Parking

Solve.

John and his children went to the zoo. He parked his car in the lot from 10:15 A.M. to 1:45 P.M. Zoo admission is $3 per person. How much did John pay to park?

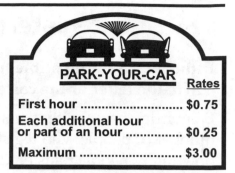

PARK-YOUR-CAR

	Rates
First hour	$0.75
Each additional hour or part of an hour	$0.25
Maximum	$3.00

Hidden Question 1 How much did John pay from 10:15 A.M. to 11:15 A.M.?

Answer _____

_____

★THINK

To solve multiple-step problems, you need to

1. Answer the Hidden Question(s)

2. Use your answer(s) to the Hidden Question(s) to answer the Final Question

Hidden Question 2 How much did he pay from 11:15 A.M. to 1:45 P.M.?

Answer _____

_____

Final Question How much did John pay to park?

Answer _____

Math Journal Can you solve this problem using mental math? Explain.

(30) The Number Line

Solve. Explain your work.

The distance between each of the marks is equal. What decimal does A represent?

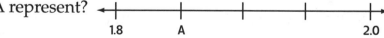

1.8   A   2.0

Answer _____

(31) Do-Gooders

Solve. Make a simpler problem.

The rules of the Do-Gooders Guild are very strict. Each junior member must do exactly (no more and no less) 8 good deeds each week. Each senior member must do exactly 12 good deeds. How many good deeds are performed by a group of 23 junior members and 26 senior members in 1 week?

You can **MAKE A SIMPLER PROBLEM** to solve this problem because

- The problem can be broken down into smaller parts

- Smaller numbers can be tried first

How to **MAKE A SIMPLER PROBLEM**

Step 1: Break apart or change the problem into problems that are simpler to solve.

Step 2: Solve the simpler problems.

Step 3: Use the answers to the simpler problems to solve the original problem.

Answer _____

Convince Me Explain how you solved the problem.

Math Journal Why is Make a Simpler Problem a useful strategy to use to solve this problem?

32) Three-Night Gig

Estimate. Use front-end estimation.
Circle the letter of the correct answer.

A guitar player performed three nights at a music hall. The first night 743 people attended the show, the second night 653 people attended, and the third night 321 people attended. About how many people attended the three shows altogether?

A. about 2,000 people

B. about 1,300 people

C. about 1,000 people

D. about 1,700 people

33) Deep-Sea Catch

Solve.

The scatter plot tells about five parties of people that went deep-sea fishing. Use the clues to decide which point on the plot shows each party. Label each point with the first letter of the party's name.

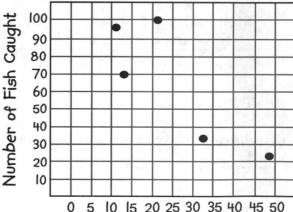

Clues

- The Perez party caught over 4 fish per person.
- The Davis party caught almost as many fish as the Perez party.
- The Hughes party caught 5 times as many fish as there were people in the party.
- The Bradford party had the most people but caught the fewest fish.
- The Chang party caught an average of one fish per person.

Math Journal How many fish did the Bradford party catch? Tell how you know.

★ **THINK**

What number pair does each point represent?

(34) Work Schedule

Solve.

Karla works 3 weekdays from 9 A.M. to 5 P.M., and on Saturday from 4 P.M. to 10 P.M. On Sundays she works from 1 P.M. to 6 P.M. How many hours does Karla work in a week?

Hidden Question 1 How many hours does Karla work altogether, in 3 weekdays?

Answer _____

Hidden Question 2 How many hours does Karla work on Saturdays?

Answer _____

Hidden Question 3 How many hours does Karla work on Sundays?

Answer _____

Final Question How many hours does Karla work in a week?

Answer _____

(35) Time for Change

Solve. Explain your work.

Mrs. Diaz did an activity with her students. One at a time, students were to give her change for a half-dollar without using pennies. No student could use the same set of coins as another student. How many students will be able to give her change?

Answer _____

Math Journal How many ways could the students give Mrs. Diaz change for a quarter using dimes, nickels, and pennies? List the ways.

36 What's for Lunch?

Solve. Make an organized list.

For lunch, you always have a drink, a sandwich, salad or soup, and a dessert. How many different lunches can you order?

Drinks	
Mineral Water	$0.85
Milk	$0.85
Juice	$1.25
Soup and Salad	
Soup	$1.25
Salad	$1.95
Sandwiches	
Hamburger	$1.85
Fish	$2.10
Chicken	$2.50
Dessert	
Pie	$1.50
Ice Cream	$0.75
Yogurt	$0.95

You can **MAKE AN ORGANIZED LIST** to solve this problem because

• You are asked to find combinations of two or more items

• There are enough items that organizing the list is helpful

How to **MAKE AN ORGANIZED LIST**

Step 1: Identify the items to be combined.

Step 2: Pick one item. Make an orderly list of all the combinations that include the item.

Step 3: Repeat Step 2 until you have found all the combinations of items.

Answer _____

Convince Me Explain how you solved the problem.

Math Journal Why is Make an Organized List a good strategy to use to solve this problem?

(37) Around Campus

Estimate. Use clustering.
Circle the letter of the correct answer.

A university campus has sides that are 4,456 feet, 4,193 feet, 4,564 feet, and 4,234 feet long. About how many feet is the perimeter of the campus?

A. about 17,200 feet

B. about 4,300 feet

C. about 18,490,000 feet

D. about 21,500 feet

Math Journal How did you choose the number with which you replaced each addend?

★ THINK

Clustering is one way to estimate. Replace each number with the same number. Choose a number that is close to the original numbers and easy to use. Then, multiply to estimate the total.

Example
132 + 129 + 131 + 133

Replace each number with 130. There are 4 numbers.

So, 4 × 130 = 520.

132 + 129 + 131 + 133 is about 520.

TEST TIP

Try working backward from an answer.

(38) Lots of Wheels

Solve.

The scatter plot tells about five cities and the number of bikes in each city. Use the clues to decide which point on the plot shows each city. Label each point with the first letter of the city's name.

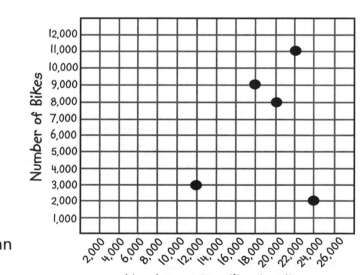

Clues

• Mountainside has 3,000 fewer bikes than Prunedale.

• Little Valley has 3 times as many bikes as Applegrove.

• The ratio of families to bikes in Prunedale is 2 to 1.

• Applegrove has 12,000 families.

• Fort Sanders has the most families and the fewest bikes.

★ THINK

What number pair does each point represent?

39 Weekend Savings

Solve.

Dora makes a collect call to her parents every week. Dora and her parents usually talk for 15 minutes. How much would Dora's parents save if she made her 15-minute call on the weekend instead of during the week?

Collect Calls	First 3 Minutes	Each Additional Minute
Monday–Friday	$2.15	$0.35
Saturday–Sunday	$2.05	$0.15

⭐**THINK**

To solve multiple-step problems, you need to

1. Answer the Hidden Question(s)

2. Use your answer(s) to the Hidden Question(s) to answer the Final Question

Hidden Question 1 How much does a 15-minute call cost during the week?

Answer _____

_____

Hidden Question 2 How much does a 15-minute call cost on the weekend?

Answer _____

Final Question How much money would Dora's parents save if she called on the weekend rather than during the week?

Answer _____

Math Journal Explain another way you could have solved this problem.

40 Carnival Time

Solve. Explain your work.

Bonnie sold $\frac{3}{6}$ of the raffle tickets for the school carnival. David sold $\frac{2}{8}$ of the tickets, and Jennie sold the rest. Did Bonnie sell more tickets by herself than David and Jennie sold together?

Answer _____

41 Be a Good Sport!

Solve. Use logical reasoning.

Wendall, Luz, Chen, and Ping each have a special sport. One of them plays basketball every day, one plays racquetball five nights a week, one loves baseball, and one coaches a tennis team. Neither Chen nor Wendall plays basketball. Luz loves her coaching job. Chen plays an outside sport. What is each person's special sport?

You can **USE LOGICAL REASONING** to solve this problem because

• There is something you know about each person

• You can use the information you know to help you find the information you don't know

How to **USE LOGICAL REASONING**

Step 1: Make an organized list or chart of the facts you know.

Step 2: Use reasoning to decide what each fact means.

Step 3: Use reasoning and the meaning of each fact to find the answer.

Answer _____

_____

Convince Me Explain how you solved the problem.

Math Journal How did you organize the clues in the problem?

Buying and Selling

REMEMBER

Rounding numbers to the nearest 10, 100, or 1,000 is one way to estimate.

Estimate. Use rounding.
Circle the letter of the correct answer.

Jamie's family bought a house for $213,350 in 2000. In 2003, they moved, and sold the house for $234,729. About how much more did Jamie's family sell the house for than they bought it for?

A.   about $220.00

B.   about $20,000

C.   about $12,000

D.   about $440,000

 Fun Park Data

Solve.

The tables show data about the new fun park in town. Study the data in the tables. Then decide which graph matches each data table. Label the axes of each graph to show your choices. (*Hint:* K *means* thousand.)

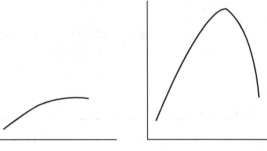

THINK

Look closely at the numbers in each table and think about how they change. Then decide which graph shows this change.

Month	March	April	May	June	July	August	Sept.	Oct.
People Riding New Coaster	10K	20K	30K	35K	37K	38K	37K	36K

Month	March	April	May	June	July	August	Sept.	Oct.
People Visiting Park	30K	65K	100K	150K	160K	175K	90K	50K

Math Journal What does the highest point in the graph on the right represent? Explain.

(44) Lunch Punch

THINK

To solve multiple-step problems, you need to

1. Answer the Hidden Question(s)

2. Use your answer(s) to the Hidden Question(s) to answer the Final Question

Solve.

Tony is planning a business luncheon for his company. There will be 48 guests at the luncheon. Each guest will get a 6-ounce glass of fruit punch. How many quarts of punch should Tony buy? (*Hint: There are 32 ounces in a quart.*)

Hidden Question How many ounces of punch should Tony buy?

Answer _____

Final Question How many quarts of punch should Tony buy?

Answer _____

Math Journal What is the divisor that is used to answer the Final Question? Explain.

(45) The Ferris Wheel

TEST TIP

Cross out extra information in the problem.

Solve. Explain your work.

Mr. Kelligan wants to know how many empty seats there are on the Ferris wheel. He counts 20 people and notices that 1 out of every 3 seats is empty. Only one person is in each seat. Two workers operate the Ferris wheel. How many empty seats are on the Ferris wheel?

Answer _____

(46) Chip and Chuck

Solve. Use Try, Check, and Revise.

Chip and Chuck had 35 peanut shells. They took the peanuts out of the shells and placed them in two piles—one pile for doubles (2 peanuts in a shell) and one pile for triples (3 peanuts in a shell). They counted 78 peanuts. How many of their peanut shells were doubles?

You can use **TRY, CHECK, AND REVISE** to solve this problem because

- Two numbers are being combined to find a total
- You need to find the numbers that are being combined

How to use **TRY, CHECK, AND REVISE**

Step 1: Make a reasonable first try.

Step 2: Check using information given in the problem.

Step 3: Use the first try to make a reasonable second try.

Step 4: Keep trying and checking until you get the answer.

Answer _____

Convince Me Explain how you solved the problem.

Math Journal How did you use your first try to make a better second try?

(47) Auto Shopper

Estimate. Use compatible numbers.
Circle the letter of the correct answer.

A new car costs $17,789. The customer gets a $1,250 rebate. About how much did the car cost the customer after the rebate?

A. about $16,500

B. about $19,000

C. about $22,250

D. about $5,500

(48) Take Me Out to the Ballgame

Solve.

The tables show data about food sales at a Little League Park. Study the data in the tables. Then decide which graph matches each data table. Label the axes of each graph to show your choices.

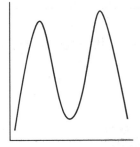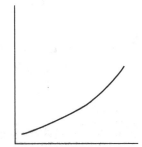

Temperature at Game Time	50°	55°	60°	65°	70°	75°	80°	85°	90°
Number of Fruit Bars Sold	3	2	10	30	50	135	190	200	210

Time of Game Start	10 A.M.	11 A.M.	12 P.M.	1 P.M.	2 P.M.	3 P.M.	4 P.M.	5 P.M.	6 P.M.	7 P.M.	8 P.M.
Number of Hot Dogs Sold	5	100	200	150	80	40	30	125	250	180	35

Math Journal About how many fruit bars would be sold when the temperature is 88°?

(49) Scented Savings

★THINK

To solve multiple-step problems, you need to

1. Answer the Hidden Question(s)

2. Use your answer(s) to the Hidden Question(s) to answer the Final Question

Solve.

Josephine wants to buy the perfume that is the better buy. Sweet Paradise costs $17.50 for a 3-ounce bottle. Simply Heavenly costs $22.50 for a 4-ounce bottle. Which perfume should she buy? About how much will she save per ounce?

Hidden Question 1 How much does 1 ounce of Sweet Paradise cost?

Answer _____

Hidden Question 2 How much does 1 ounce of Simply Heavenly cost?

Answer _____

Final Question Which perfume should she buy? About how much will she save per ounce?

Answer _____

_____

Math Journal Why is it necessary to find the per-ounce cost of each perfume?

(50) Health Crunch

Solve. Explain your work.

Antoine baked a batch of oatmeal clusters. He ate $\frac{1}{4}$ of the clusters on Monday. He ate some clusters on Tuesday. On Wednesday, 16 clusters or $\frac{2}{3}$ of the clusters he baked, were still left. How many clusters did Antoine bake? How many clusters did Antoine eat on Monday?

Answer _____

(51) **From High to Low**

Solve. Make a graph.

Mrs. Lowe just finished grading the last test of the year. Her students' grades are listed to the right. Mrs. Lowe uses a grading scale. A grade in the 90s is an A, a grade in the 80s is a B, a grade in the 70s is a C, a grade in the 60s is a D, and anything below 60 is an F. Which two grades occur most frequently?

Grades:
70, 54, 96, 88, 25, 97,
65, 83, 99, 75, 73, 82,
55, 34, 97, 87, 89, 95,
68, 72, 84, 71, 36, 78

 TEST TIP

Think about what problem-solving strategies might help you.

You can **MAKE A GRAPH** to solve this problem because

- Data for an event is given

- The question in the problem can be answered by visualizing the data in the graph

How to **MAKE A GRAPH**

Step 1: Set up and label the graph.

Step 2: Enter known data.

Step 3: Analyze the graph to solve the problem.

Answer _____

Convince Me Explain how you solved the problem.

Math Journal What kind of graph did you make? What other kind of graph could you have made? Explain.

(52) Cable Costs

Estimate. Use front-end estimation.
Circle the letter of the correct answer.

Vision Cable charges $54.95 per month or $599.40 a year for cable service. Their competitor, Wired Cable, charges $39.99 per month or $443.88 per year for cable service. On the yearly plan, about how much less does Wired Cable cost per year than Vision Cable?

A.   about $1,030.00

B.   about $200.00

C.   about $160.00

D.   about $100.00

⭐ **THINK**

Using front-end digits is one way to estimate. Add, subtract, multiply, or divide the front-end digits. Then, adjust the estimate by looking at the digits to the right.

Example

967 − 391 is about
900 − 300 = 600.

67 < 91 so,
967 − 391 is less than 600.

(53) Wiggly Creatures

Solve.

Brian and Sal each have a collection of wigglies. The wigglies are worms, frogs, and lizards. Use the clues to find out how many of each kind of wiggly the boys have. Write the number of each kind.

⭐ **THINK**

Start with what you know for sure.

Brian's Box of Wigglies	**Sal's Box of Wigglies**
Clues • 8 wigglies in all	**Clues** • 9 wigglies in all
• 2 worms	• 4 worms
• 2 more frogs than lizards	• 1 fewer lizard than worms
Worms _____	Worms _____
Frogs _____	Frogs _____
Lizards _____	Lizards _____

Math Journal Check your work by making a list of each group of wigglies. Use *W* for worms, *F* for frogs, and *L* for lizards.

(54) Party On

Write the Hidden Question. Then solve.

Hamburger Heaven was hired to provide food for a school party. Each item was sold for $0.65. How much money did Hamburger Heaven make at the party?

Hidden Question _____

Answer _____

_____

Final Question How much money did Hamburger Heaven make at the party?

Answer _____

_____

Math Journal Did Hamburger Heaven make more money selling pie or selling hamburgers? Explain how you know the answer without doing any computation.

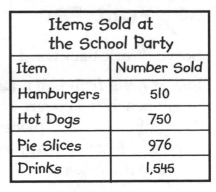

Items Sold at the School Party	
Item	Number Sold
Hamburgers	510
Hot Dogs	750
Pie Slices	976
Drinks	1,545

★**THINK**

To solve multiple-step problems, you need to

1. Answer the Hidden Question(s)

2. Use your answer(s) to the Hidden Question(s) to answer the Final Question

(55) Pets Galore

Solve. Explain your work.

Joanna's class took a survey to find the number of pets owned by each student in the class. The results of the survey are below. What is the mode of the data?

Student	Number of Pets	Student	Number of Pets
Joanna	1	Jeremy	2
Mattie	3	Antoine	4
José	2	Barry	2
Donald	2	Jackie	4
Ricky	1	Sandy	1
Doris	2	Monica	3
June	4	Suzanne	2
Devon	1	Shanika	1
Tamika	2	Larry	2
Nancy	2	Sandra	1
Tom	4	Frankie	5
Kelly	2	Deepak	2

Answer _____

56 Fruit Fan

Solve. Work backward.

Josh is a big fruit eater. Last weekend he ate twice as
many peaches as pears and 6 fewer bananas than peaches.
Altogether, he ate 7 pieces of fruit that were bananas or
apples. If Josh ate 3 apples, how many pieces of fruit did
he eat last weekend?

> You can **WORK BACKWARD** to solve this problem
> because
>
> • An end amount and some information about
>   each unknown amount are given
>
> • Each unknown amount can be found by
>   comparing it to the end amount or to
>   other amounts
>
> How to **WORK BACKWARD**
>
> **Step 1:** Identify what is unknown.
>
> **Step 2:** Draw a picture or describe how each
> amount compares to other amounts, starting with
> what is unknown at the beginning.
>
> **Step 3:** Work backward from the end, using the
> opposite of each change.

Answer _____

Convince Me Explain how you solved the problem.

Math Journal How many steps did it take to solve the problem?

57 BUSI-ER

Patients Admitted	
2 P.M.–3 P.M.	13
3 P.M.–4 P.M.	15
4 P.M.–5 P.M.	17
5 P.M.–6 P.M.	12
6 P.M.–7 P.M.	17

Estimate. Use clustering.
Circle the letter of the correct answer.

The emergency room at the hospital was very busy on Friday. Use the table to find about how many patients were admitted on Friday between 2 P.M. and 7 P.M.

A. about 15 patients

B. about 40 patients

C. about 64 patients

D. about 75 patients

Math Journal Do you think your estimate is very close to the actual answer? Explain.

REMEMBER
Clustering is one way to estimate. Replace each number with the same number. Choose a number that is close to the original numbers. Then, multiply to estimate the total.

58 Fruit Counts

THINK
You can use the clues in any order.

Solve.

Mary and Pam each have a bag of fruit. In their bags are apples, oranges, and bananas. Use the clues to find out how many of each kind of fruit the girls have. Write the number of each kind.

TEST TIP
Draw a picture to help you solve the problem.

Mary's Bag of Fruit	Pam's Bag of Fruit
Clues • 6 apples	**Clues** • 4 fewer bananas than oranges
• 2 more bananas than oranges	• 10 pieces of fruit in all
• 12 pieces of fruit in all	• 3 times as many oranges as apples
Apples _____	Apples _____
Bananas _____	Bananas _____
Oranges _____	Oranges _____

(59) Old-Time Prices

Write the Hidden Question. Then solve.

The sign shows the prices of items people could buy in 1850. What is the total cost of 3 blankets, 2 sacks of flour, 10 pounds of rice, and 1 bushel of beans?

Hidden Question _____

_____

Answer _____

_____

_____

Final Question What is the total cost of all the items?

Answer _____

_____

ESTABLISHED 1850

GENERAL STORE

Blanket	$1.70
Bucket	$0.30
Cloth	$0.25/yd
Beans	$1.50/bushel
Flour	$3.00/sack
Rice	$0.15/lb
Salt	$0.02/lb

⭐**THINK**

To solve multiple-step problems, you need to

1. Answer the Hidden Question(s)

2. Use your answer(s) to the Hidden Question(s) to answer the Final Question

(60) Fellow Factors

Solve. Explain your work.

If 20 is a factor of a number, what other numbers must also be factors of that number?

Answer _____

_____

Math Journal How do you know your conclusion works for all numbers of which 20 is a factor?

61 High and Higher

Solve. Write an equation.

The height of Angel Falls in Venezuela added to the height of King George Falls in Guyana is 4,812 feet. Angel Falls is 1,612 feet higher than King George Falls. How high is King George Falls?

You can **WRITE AN EQUATION** to solve this problem because

- You need to find a quantity that is unknown
- There is a relationship between the unknown quantity and other quantities that involves a mathematical operation

How to **WRITE AN EQUATION**

Step 1: Show the main idea of the problem.

Step 2: Decide which operation goes with the main idea.

Step 3: Use a letter to show what you are trying to find.

Step 4: Write and solve the equation.

Answer _____

Convince Me Explain how you solved the problem.

Math Journal How can you check your answer?

62 Reading Record

TEST TIP

Try working backward from an answer.

Estimate. Use rounding.
Circle the letter of the correct answer.

A class of 19 students read a total of 2,553 pages of science material during the 2004–2005 school year. Each student read about the same number of pages. About how many pages did each student read?

REMEMBER

Rounding numbers to the nearest 10, 100, or 1,000 is one way to estimate.

A. about 25 pages

B. about 50 pages

C. about 80 pages

D. about 120 pages

63 Fishy Problem

★**THINK**

Start with what you know for sure.

Solve.

Rudy and Jim each have a bowl of fish. The fish are guppies, neons, and swordtails. Use the clues to find out how many of each kind of fish the boys have. Write the number of each kind.

Rudy's Bowl of Fish	**Jim's Bowl of Fish**
Clues • 14 fish in all	**Clues** • 6 swordtails
• 2 guppies	• Half as many neons as guppies
• Twice as many neons as swordtails	• 15 fish in all
Guppies _____	Guppies _____
Neons _____	Neons _____
Swordtails _____	Swordtails _____

Math Journal Tell how you know there is only one solution for each bowl of fish.

(64) Troop of Visitors

Write the Hidden Questions. Then solve.

A Troop Leader buys one single-day amusement park ticket for each of the 12 Lion Group members in his troop, and one two-day ticket for each of the 10 Grizzly Group members in his troop. How much do the tickets cost altogether?

★THINK

To solve multiple-step problems, you need to

1. Answer the Hidden Question(s)

2. Use your answer(s) to the Hidden Question(s) to answer the Final Question

Hidden Question 1 _____

Answer _____

_____

Hidden Question 2 _____

Answer _____

Final Question How much do the tickets cost altogether?

Answer _____

(65) Tiles × Tiles

Solve. Explain your work.

The figure at the right has 2 rows of 3 tiles each. We say the dimensions of this rectangle are 2 × 3. Find all the possible dimensions for rectangles with the following number of tiles. (*Hint: 2 × 3 is the same as 3 × 2.*)

1. 30 tiles
2. 36 tiles
3. 17 tiles

Answer _____

_____

Math Journal What is the relationship between the dimensions of each possible rectangle for each number of tiles and the factors for each number of tiles?

(66) Beach Ball Toss

Solve. Make a simpler problem.

Rockytop School is holding a contest to raise money for the school band. In each match in the contest, pairs of students will toss a wet beach ball back and forth until one of the students misses the beach ball and is out of the contest. Players will continue to play against other players until they miss the beach ball. Thirty-two students have entered the contest. How many matches need to be played in order to determine a champion?

You can **MAKE A SIMPLER PROBLEM** to solve this problem because

• The problem can be broken down into smaller parts that are simpler to solve

How to **MAKE A SIMPLER PROBLEM**

Step 1: Break apart or change the problem into problems that are simpler to solve.

Step 2: Solve the simpler problems.

Step 3: Use the answers to the simpler problems to solve the original problem.

Answer _____

Convince Me Explain how you solved the problem.

Math Journal Why is "Make a Simpler Problem" a useful strategy for solving this problem?

(67) Lap It Up!

Estimate. Use compatible numbers.
Circle the letter of the correct answer.

Marie is on the track team. She runs 14 laps a day around her high school track for practice. How many laps has she run after 123 days of practice?

A. about 1,500 laps

B. about 150 laps

C. about 15,000 laps

D. about 4,000 laps

(68) By the Bunch

Solve.

Amanda and Shannon each have a bunch of flowers. The flowers are daisies, roses, and irises. Use the clues to find out how many of each kind of flower the girls have. Write the number of each kind.

Amanda's Bunch of Flowers	**Shannon's Bunch of Flowers**
Clues • 18 flowers in all	**Clues** • $\frac{1}{3}$ as many roses as irises
• 2 irises	• 20 flowers in all
• 3 times as many daisies as roses	• 8 daisies
Daisies _____	Daisies _____
Roses _____	Roses _____
Irises _____	Irises _____

Math Journal Check your work by making a list of each bunch of flowers. Use *D* for daisies, *R* for roses, and *I* for irises.

(69) Biker Deal

Write the Hidden Questions. Then solve.

Lionel bought a bike for $40. He bought $20 worth of new parts and fixed it up. He sold the bike for $130. He used the money to buy another bike for $60. He bought $25 worth of new parts and fixed it up. He sold that bike for $150. How much profit did Lionel make altogether?

Hidden Question 1 _____

Answer _____

Hidden Question 2 _____

Answer _____

Final Question How much profit did Lionel make altogether?

Answer _____

Math Journal Can you find another way to solve this problem? Explain.

(70) The Flower Garden

Solve. Explain your work.

Monica has 12 sections of garden fencing. Each section is 3 feet long. She is going to put a rectangular flower garden next to the house and enclose the garden on three sides with the fencing. The house will enclose the fourth side. What is the area of the greatest flower garden Monica can create with the fencing?

Answer _____

71 Design It

Solve. Use objects.

Beverly is making a design out of color tiles. The design is a
4-color rectangle. Half of the tiles she is using are red, $\frac{1}{3}$ are blue,
$\frac{1}{8}$ are yellow, and one tile is green. How many tiles are red?

You can **USE OBJECTS** to solve this problem
because

- The numbers in the problem are small

- There is something in the problem that you can
  show with objects

Answer _____

Convince Me Explain how you solved the problem.

Math Journal How many tiles are yellow? How many tiles are
blue? Explain.

(72) Through the Years

Estimate. Use front-end estimation.
Circle the letter of the correct answer.

Mr. Polanski teaches an average of 127 students a year. He has been a teacher for 33 years. About how many students has Mr. Polanski taught altogether?

A. about 1,300 students

B. about 3,090 students

C. about 3,900 students

D. about 39,000 students

Math Journal Which answer choices are unreasonable? Explain.

(73) How Many of Each?

Solve.

Liza and Donna each have a bunch of balloons. There are red, green, and yellow balloons. Use the clues to find out how many of each color balloon the girls have. Write the number of each kind.

Liza's Bunch of Balloons	Donna's Bunch of Balloons
Clues • 10 red balloons • 20 balloons in all • 4 times as many green balloons as yellow balloons	**Clues** • $\frac{1}{4}$ as many yellow balloons as green balloons • 4 red balloons • 24 balloons in all
Red _____	Red _____
Green _____	Green _____
Yellow _____	Yellow _____

(74) Pony Problem

Write the Hidden Question. Then solve.

Carrie's pony is 11 hands high. How tall is her pony in feet and inches? *(Hint: 1 hand = 4 inches)*

Hidden Question _____

Answer _____

Final Question How tall is the pony in feet and inches?

Answer _____

_____

(75) Name That Fraction

Solve. Explain your work.

Write the approximate value of the shaded part of the figure as a fraction of the whole figure.

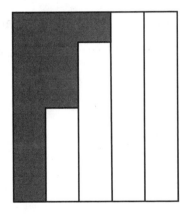

Answer _____

Math Journal What part of the figure is not shaded? Explain.

76 Elia's Fence

TEST TIP
Draw a picture to help you solve the problem.

Solve. Make a simpler problem.

Elia built three corrals that are side by side. Each corral is a square. The middle corral shares one side with the corral on the left and one side with the corral on the right. Elia used 6 vertical posts for each side of each corral. How many posts did Elia use in all?

You can **MAKE A SIMPLER PROBLEM** to solve this problem because

• The problem can be broken down into smaller parts

Answer _____

Convince Me Explain how you solved the problem.

Math Journal How did drawing a picture help you solve a simpler problem?

77 Raspberry Pickin'

Berries Picked	
Monday	63 pints
Tuesday	69 pints
Wednesday	61 pints
Thursday	67 pints
Friday	66 pints

Estimate. Use clustering.
Circle the letter of the correct answer.

Baram has a summer job picking berries. He works five days in a row. The table shows how much he picked. About how many pints of berries did he pick in five days?

A. about 250 pints

B. about 325 pints

C. about 390 pints

D. about 535 pints

REMEMBER

Clustering is one way to estimate. Replace each number with the same number. Choose a number that is close to the original numbers. Then, multiply to estimate the total.

78 Find the Balance

★THINK

How many marbles must be in all the bags? How many marbles must be in each bag?

The pans in each picture are balanced. Read the balancing rules. Then find the number of marbles in each bag.

Balancing Rules

• A balance must have the same number of marbles on each side.

• On each balance, all bags must have the same number of marbles.

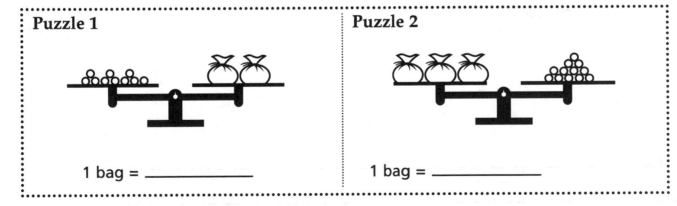

Puzzle 1

1 bag = _____

Puzzle 2

1 bag = _____

Math Journal Tell about your thinking when you solved each puzzle.

(79) What's Left?

Write the Hidden Question. Then solve.

Pepe earned $137.89 working during spring vacation. He spent $21.15 to fix his bike and $15.50 on a birthday present for his brother. How much money does Pepe have left?

Hidden Question _____

Answer _____

Final Question How much money does Pepe have left?

Answer _____

(80) A Fruitful Job

Solve. Explain your work.

Eva worked at an orchard during the summer. The fruit inspectors throw out about 2 out of every 7 pieces of fruit because they are not good enough to sell. About what percentage of the fruit cannot be sold? Round to the nearest whole percent. Out of 200 pieces of fruit, about how many pieces cannot be sold?

Answer _____

_____

Math Journal Out of 200 pieces of fruit, how many pieces can be sold? Explain.

81 A Hairy Job

Solve. Look for a pattern.

Last Saturday, Terry worked in a dog grooming salon. His employer agreed to pay him $0.01 for the first dog he brushed, $0.02 for the second dog he brushed, $0.04 for the third dog he brushed, $0.08 for the fourth dog he brushed, and so on until he had brushed 12 dogs. How much was he paid for brushing the twelfth dog?

You can **LOOK FOR A PATTERN** to solve this problem

- Because something repeats and changes

- What repeats or changes does so in the same way every time

Answer _____

Convince Me Explain how you solved the problem.

Math Journal Do you think Terry was paid well for brushing the 12 dogs? Explain.

(82) Tall Crops

Estimate. Use rounding.
Circle the letter of the correct answer.

REMEMBER

Rounding numbers to the nearest 10, 100, or 1,000 is one way to estimate.

Each year a tree farm plants trees. In 2002, the farm planted 981 trees. In 2003, the farm planted 873 trees, and in 2004, the farm planted 1,298 trees. About how many trees did the farm plant altogether in those three years?

A. about 315 trees

B. about 2,000 trees

C. about 2,200 trees

D. about 3,000 trees

Math Journal Did the farm plant more trees altogether in 2003 and 2004 or in 2002 and 2004? Find the answer without adding. Explain.

(83) Balancing Act

The pans in each picture are balanced. Read the balancing rules. Then find the number of marbles in each bag.

⭐**THINK**

Could the pans still be balanced if some marbles are removed from each side?

Balancing Rules

• A balance must have the same number of marbles on each side.

• On each balance, all bags must have the same number of marbles.

Puzzle 1

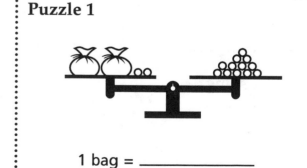

1 bag = _____

Puzzle 2

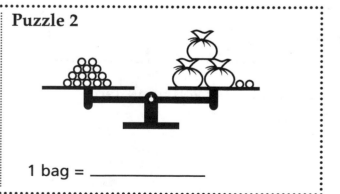

1 bag = _____

(84) It's Raining!

Average Annual Rainfall (in inches)	
Athens, Greece	14.6
Lagos, Nigeria	59.3
Lima, Peru	0.2
Sydney, Australia	4.64

Write the Hidden Question. Then solve.

How much greater is the average annual rainfall in Lagos, Nigeria, than in Athens, Greece? Give your answer in feet and inches.

Hidden Question _____

_____

Answer _____

_____

Final Question How much greater in feet and inches is the average annual rainfall in Lagos, Nigeria, than in Athens, Greece?

Answer _____

_____

⭐**THINK**

To solve multiple-step problems, you need to

1. Answer the Hidden Question(s)

2. Use your answer(s) to the Hidden Question(s) to answer the Final Question

TEST TIP

Circle information in the table that you will use to solve the problem.

(85) Getting Close

Solve. Explain your work.

Write the digits 4, 5, 6, 7, 8, or 9 in the boxes to the right to see how close you can get to a product of 40,000, without going over 40,000. Each digit may be used only once.

☐ ☐ ☐ ☐
✗   ☐

Answer _____

Math Journal How close is the product you found to 40,000? Explain.

86 Weighty Melons

Solve. Draw a picture.

A farmer has 8 melons. The weight of 7 of the melons is exactly the same, but one melon is a little heavier than the others. Using a pan balance, how can the farmer find the heavier melon by weighing melons exactly two times?

You can **DRAW A PICTURE** to solve this problem because

- The problem describes some action in a physical sense

- It can help you visualize the problem

Answer _____

Convince Me Explain how you solved the problem.

Math Journal How did drawing a picture help you to solve the problem?

(87) Health Craze

Estimate. Use compatible numbers.
Circle the letter of the correct answer.

Three weeks ago a new health club opened in
Binghamton. The first week, 552 people joined the
club. The second week, 237 people joined, and the
third week, 207 people joined. About how many
people joined the club during its first three weeks?

A. about 440 people

B. about 600 people

C. about 900 people

D. about 1,000 people

REMEMBER

Using compatible numbers
is one way to estimate.
Replace numbers with
numbers that are close
and easy to use in your
head.

(88) Marble Match

The pans in each picture are balanced. Read the balancing
rules. Then find the number of marbles in each bag.

Balancing Rules

• A balance must have the same number of marbles
on each side.

• On each balance, all bags must have the same
number of marbles.

★**THINK**

Could the pans still be
balanced if some marbles
are removed from each
side? Could the pans be
balanced if some bags are
removed from each side?

Puzzle 1	Puzzle 2
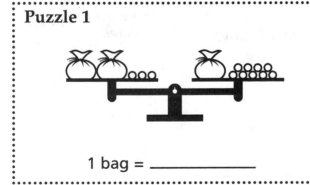	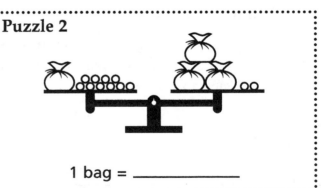
1 bag = _____	1 bag = _____

Math Journal Tell about your thinking when you solved each puzzle.

(89) Learning Languages

Solve.

There are 20 students in each class at a language school. There are 3 classes on Monday, 3 classes on Wednesday, and 3 classes on Friday. Each class meets 1 night a week for 3 months. There are 4 three-month sessions in each school year. Each student takes only 1 class per year. In one year, how many people take a class at the language school?

Answer _____

Math Journal If you didn't know that each student only takes one class per year, could you solve the problem? Explain.

(90) Small Servings

Solve. Explain your work.

Meena made 12 cups of gelatin. She divided the gelatin into equal servings. Each serving was $\frac{2}{3}$ of a cup. How many servings did Meena make?

TEST TIP

Check if your answer makes sense.

Answer _____

91 Raising Guppies

Solve. Work backward.

Ms. Mates raises guppies. One day she donated 20 of her guppies to a school. Then, she bought the same number of guppies as the number that was left at home. She divided all the guppies into equal groups and gave them to 6 friends. She gave each friend 15 guppies. How many guppies did she have to start with?

You can **WORK BACKWARD** to solve this problem because

- You start with an unknown amount that changes in ways that are described

- An end amount is given

Answer _____

Convince Me Explain how you solved the problem.

Math Journal Explain why you chose the operations you used to solve the problem.

92 Pumping Iron

Estimate. Use front-end estimation.
Circle the letter of the correct answer.

Four boys are on a weight-lifting team. Lenny can bench press 223 pounds. Brad can bench press 117 pounds. Haitham can bench press 205 pounds. Richie can bench press 315 pounds. About how many pounds can the team bench press altogether?

A. about 425 pounds

B. about 700 pounds

C. about 1,200 pounds

D. about 860 pounds

Math Journal Is your unadjusted estimate close to your adjusted estimate? Explain.

REMEMBER

Using the front-end digits is one way to estimate. Add, subtract, multiply, or divide the front-end digits. Then, adjust the estimate by looking at the digits to the right.

TEST TIP

Cross out unreasonable answer choices.

93 Marble-ous

The pans in each picture are balanced. Read the balancing rules. Then find the number of marbles in each bag.

Balancing Rules

• A balance must have the same number of marbles on each side.

• On each balance, all bags must have the same number of marbles.

• The boxes of marbles are labeled to show how many marbles are in each box.

★**THINK**

Could the pans still be balanced if some bags are removed from each side? Could the pans still be balanced if some of the marbles in the box on each side are removed?

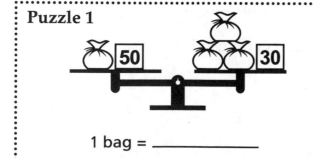

Puzzle 1

1 bag = _____

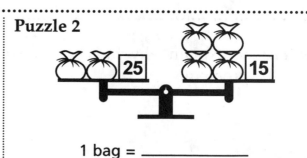

Puzzle 2

1 bag = _____

(94) Decisions, Decisions

Solve.

You want to buy a home computer. The computer costs $875 if you pay the entire amount at once. If you pay over time, you have to put $100 down and pay $76.25 a month for one year. Which method of payment costs less? How much less?

Answer _____

Math Journal Why might a person choose to pay for the computer monthly rather than all at once?

(95) Power Up

Solve. Explain your work.

What number do you get when you multiply 24.0567 by 10, then multiply the product by 10, then multiply that product by 10, and so on?

Answer _____

96 Ocean Stats

Solve. Write an equation.

If the average depth of the Arctic Ocean is tripled, the result is 114 meters (m) more than 3,000 m. What is the average depth of the Arctic Ocean?

> You can **WRITE AN EQUATION** to solve this problem because
>
> • You need to find a quantity that is unknown
>
> • There is a relationship between the unknown quantity and other quantities that involves a mathematical operation

Answer _____

Convince Me Explain how you solved the problem.

Math Journal What different equation could you have written to solve the problem? (*Hint: Use a different operation in your equation.*)

(97) Food Funds

Estimate. Use rounding.
Circle the letter of the correct answer.

The pie chart to the right shows how much Theresa spent on food during her first semester at college. About how much did she spend on food altogether during her first semester?

A. about $350

B. about $1,100

C. about $1,400

D. about $2,000

REMEMBER

Rounding numbers to the nearest 10, 100, or 1,000 is one way to estimate.

(98) More Marbles

The pans in each picture are balanced. Read the balancing rules. Then find the number of marbles in each bag.

Balancing Rules

• A balance must have the same number of marbles on each side.

• On each balance, all bags must have the same number of marbles.

• The boxes of marbles are labeled to show how many marbles are in each box.

⭐**THINK**

Could the pans still be balanced if some bags are removed from each side? Could the pans still be balanced if some of the marbles in boxes on each side are removed?

Puzzle 1

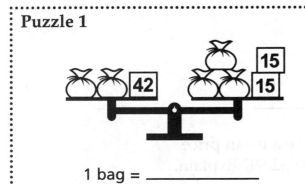

1 bag = _____

Puzzle 2

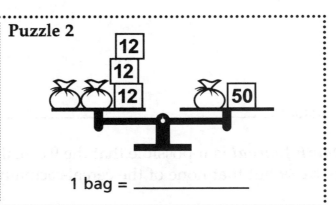

1 bag = _____

Math Journal Tell about your thinking when you solved each puzzle.

99 Busloads

Solve.

TEST TIP
Cross out extra information in the problem.

Today, 1,105 students are going to a concert. The school has arranged for 5 buses to take the students from school to the concert arena. Each bus holds 45 passengers. The concert arena is 6 miles from the school. How many trips will each bus have to make to bring all the students to the concert?

Answer _____

100 Serious Cereal

Solve. Explain your work.

A store sells 9 different brands of cereal. The mean price for the cereals is $2.89. No two prices are the same. List 9 possible prices for the cereal, one price for each brand. Make sure that each price is a reasonable price for a box of cereal.

Answer _____

Math Journal Is it possible that the 9 cereals have a mean price of $2.89 but that none of the cereals actually cost $2.89? Explain.

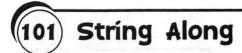

(101) String Along

Solve. Make a simpler problem.

Kate used pieces of string and 9 nails to make a string web. She
ran a piece of string from each nail to each of the other nails.
How many pieces of string did she use?

Answer _____

Convince Me Explain how you solved the problem.

Math Journal Did you find a number pattern in the simpler
problems you solved that helped you to find the answer to the
original problem? Explain.

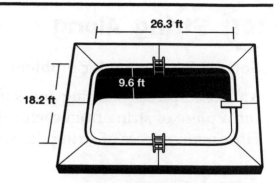

(102) Filling the Pool

Estimate. Use rounding.
Circle the letter of the correct answer.

Spring is here, and the community center needs to fill the pool with water. About how many cubic feet is the volume of the pool?

A. about 2,000 cubic feet

B. about 3,000 cubic feet

C. about 6,000 cubic feet

D. about 30,000 cubic feet

REMEMBER

Rounding numbers to the nearest 10, 100, or 1,000 is one way to estimate.

(103) Find All the Ways

Solve.

Find all the ways to put marbles in these cans and boxes to make the total shown. Use the rules below. Show the ways in the table.

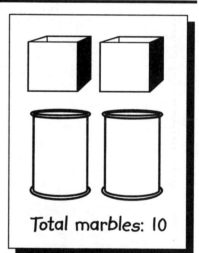

Total marbles: 10

Rules
• Each can must have the same number of marbles.
• Each box must have the same number of marbles.

Marbles in Each Can	0	1				
Marbles in Each Box						

Math Journal Tell about one way that does not work. Tell why not.

★THINK

Start like this: When there are 0 marbles in each can, is it possible to put marbles in the boxes so the total is 10? Now try 1 marble in each can.

104 **A Reason to Party**

Solve.

There were 347 people at a charity dinner party. Each guest paid $150 to the charity to attend the party. The expenses for the party were $5,000. How much money did the charity raise after paying expenses?

*Answer*_____

105 **Fraction Match**

Solve. Explain your work.

Match each fraction with its equivalent percent. Then write the fractions and percents in order from least to greatest.

$\frac{1}{5}$ $\frac{1}{8}$ $\frac{1}{2}$ $\frac{1}{4}$ $\frac{1}{10}$ $\frac{1}{3}$ $\frac{9}{9}$

$33\frac{1}{3}\%$ 50%   20% $12\frac{1}{2}\%$ 10%   100%   25%

Answer _____

Math Journal What are the word names of each fraction in the problem above?

(106) We All Scream for Ice Cream

Ice Cream Flavors	vanilla chocolate strawberry
Fruit	raspberries cherries bananas
Sauces	hot fudge caramel blueberry
Toppings	nuts sprinkles chocolate chips

Solve. Make an organized list.

Your class is having an ice cream sundae party. To make sure there is enough for everyone, the class has decided that each student can choose 1 ice cream flavor, 1 fruit, 1 kind of sauce, and 1 topping. How many different sundae combinations can students make?

You can **MAKE AN ORGANIZED LIST** to solve this problem because

- You are asked to find combinations of two or more items

- There are enough items that organizing the list is helpful

Answer _____

Convince Me Explain how you solved the problem.

Math Journal Why is making an organized list a good way to solve this problem?

(107) Season Premiere

Estimate. Use clustering.
Circle the letter of the correct answer.

At the beginning of a new TV season, a sitcom had about 14,056,000 viewers for the first show, about 13,678,000 viewers for the second show, and about 14,256,000 viewers for the third show. About how many viewers watched the first three shows altogether?

A. about 42,000,000 viewers

B. about 33,000,000 viewers

C. about 30,000,000 viewers

D. about 29,680,000 viewers

(108) Can Do

Solve.

Find all the ways to put marbles in these cans and boxes to make the total shown. Use the rules below. Show the ways in the table.

Rules
- Each can must have the same number of marbles.
- Each box must have the same number of marbles.

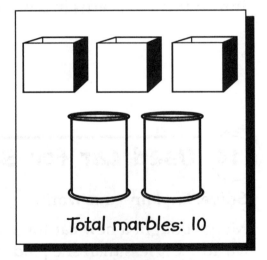

Total marbles: 10

Marbles in Each Can						
Marbles in Each Box						

Math Journal When there are 0 marbles in each box, how many marbles are in each can? Tell how you know.

★**THINK**

Start like this: When there are 0 marbles in each can, is it possible to put marbles in the boxes so the total is 10? Now try 1 marble in each can.

Solve.

Zelda earns $22 an hour as a brick layer, plus $100 per week.
Fern earns $32 an hour as a carpenter. How much more does
Fern earn in one week if they each work 40 hours?

Answer _____

Math Journal Why does it take two steps to find out how much
Zelda earns in a week, but it only takes one step to find out
how much Fern earns in a week?

Solve. Explain your work.

Marga bought a new car for $16,850. A year later she sold the
car for 20% less than she paid for it. The car had 18,452 miles
on it when she sold it. For how much did Marga sell her car?

TEST TIP

Cross out extra
information in the
problem.

Answer _____

(111) PJs for Quadruplets

Solve. Use logical reasoning.

Brian, Bennie, Bruce, and Barry are quadruplets. Each boy wears pajamas in a different favorite color. One brother wears blue. Neither Bruce nor Barry likes red. Bennie always wears green. Barry started to choose yellow, but he decided against it. What color pajamas does each boy wear?

> You can **USE LOGICAL REASONING** to solve this problem because
>
> • There is something you know about each person
>
> • You can use the information you know to help you find the information you don't know

Answer _____

_____

Convince Me Explain how you solved the problem.

Math Journal How did you keep track of the information in the problem to decide which color pajamas each boy wears?

(112) Roll Out the Carpet

Estimate. Use front-end estimation.
Circle the letter of the correct answer.

REMEMBER

Using the front-end digits is one way to estimate. Add, subtract, multiply, or divide the front-end digits. Then, adjust the estimate by looking at the digits to the right.

A decorator wants to carpet the first floor of a new building. The building is 1,347 feet long by 983 feet wide. About how many square feet of carpet does the decorator need to order?

A. about 2,200 square feet

B. about 1,200,000 square feet

C. about 400 square feet

D. about 90,000 square feet

(113) Mix and Match

Solve.

Find all the ways to put marbles in these cans and boxes to make the total shown. Use the rules below. Show the ways in the table.

Rules
- Each can must have the same number of marbles.
- Each box must have the same number of marbles.

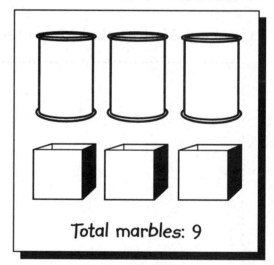

Total marbles: 9

Marbles in Each Can				
Marbles in Each Box				

Math Journal Is there a solution with 4 marbles in each can? Explain how you know.

★THINK

Start like this: When there are 0 marbles in each can, is it possible to put marbles in the boxes so the total is 9? Now try 1 marble in each can.

(114) Thousands of Pages

Solve.

Angel wrote a novel. The novel is 652 pages. Angel made 55 copies of her novel to send to publishing companies. How many reams of paper did Angel buy in order to make copies of her novel? (*Hint: A ream of paper is 500 sheets.*)

Answer _____

(115) A Weighty Matter

TEST TIP
Think about what problem-solving strategies might help you.

Solve. Explain your work.

A dime weighs 40% as much as a quarter weighs. A penny weighs 50% as much as a nickel weighs. A half dollar weighs two times as much as a quarter. A half dollar weighs 11.34 grams. How much does a dime weigh?

Answer _____

Math Journal What strategy did you use to solve this problem? Explain.

(116) Cheap Seats

Solve. Use Try, Check, and Revise.

Omar paid $50 to buy some adult tickets and some student tickets for a school play. Adult tickets are $7 each, and student tickets are $5. If he bought 8 tickets, how many adult tickets and how many student tickets did he buy?

You can use **TRY, CHECK, AND REVISE** to solve this problem because

• Some quantities are being combined to find a total

• You do not know how many of each quantity are used to get the total

Answer _____

Convince Me Explain how you solved the problem.

Math Journal How did you use Try, Check, and Revise to find the answer?

117 It's a Kick!

Estimate. Use clustering.
Circle the letter of the correct answer.

The Girls Soccer Club is buying new uniforms. Each player needs cleats, a sweatshirt, shorts, and a jersey. Find the approximate total cost of each complete uniform.

Uniforms	
Cleats	$43.95 each
Sweatshirts	$49.99 each
Shorts	$46.00 each
Jerseys	$44.50 each

A. about $180

B. about $300

C. about $141

D. about $94

REMEMBER

Clustering is one way to estimate. Replace each number with the same number. Choose a number that is close to the original numbers. Then, multiply to estimate the total.

118 Sorting It Out

Solve.

Find all the ways to put marbles in these cans and boxes to make the total shown. Use the rules below. Show the ways in the table.

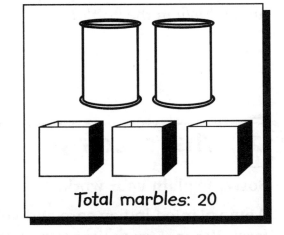

Total marbles: 20

Rules
- Each can must have the same number of marbles.
- Each box must have the same number of marbles.

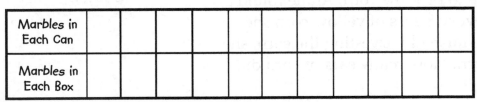

Marbles in Each Can										
Marbles in Each Box										

★THINK

Start like this: When there are 0 marbles in each can, is it possible to put marbles in the boxes so the total is 20? Now try 1 marble in each can.

Math Journal Tell about any patterns you see in the table above.

(119) A Mound of Marbles

Solve.

A 6-liter bottle is filled with marbles that are all the same size. Seventy marbles can fit in a 250-milliliter beaker. How many marbles are probably in the bottle?

Answer _____

Math Journal Why does the problem ask, "How many marbles are *probably* in the bottle?"

(120) That's Corny

Solve. Explain your work.

Annie planted Indian corn and yellow corn on her small farm. When it came time to pick the corn, Annie found 3 ears of Indian corn for every 8 ears of yellow corn she harvested. When Annie finished harvesting the corn, she had 64 ears of yellow corn. How many ears of corn did Annie harvest altogether?

TEST TIP

Look for important words that tell you what the problem is about.

Answer _____

(121) Movie Mania

Solve. Make a graph.

Mr. Fan's sixth-grade class took a survey to see how many movies the students had rented in the past month. The results of that survey are listed below. What is the mode of this data?

Students	Movies	Students	Movies	Students	Movies	Students	Movies
Bob	1	June	5	Jeremy	3	Suzanne	2
Mattie	6	Devon	10	Antoine	4	Shanika	4
José	3	Larry	12	Barry	8	Tamika	6
Donald	4	Nancy	6	Jackie	3	Sandra	7
Ricky	4	Tom	3	Sandy	8	Frankie	5
Doris	12	Kelly	5	Monica	3	Phillip	7

You can **MAKE A GRAPH** to solve this problem because

• Data for an event is given

• The question in the problem can be answered by visualizing the data in a graph

Answer _____

Convince Me Explain how you solved the problem.

Math Journal How did making a graph help you to solve this problem?

(122) Cruisin'

Estimate. Use any method you like.

A cruise ship leaves port with 1,583 pounds of fish onboard to serve the passengers. The cruise will last 5 days. There are 714 passengers onboard the ship. About how many pounds of fish are onboard for each passenger? Round your answer to the nearest pound.

TEST TIP

Cross out extra information in the problem.

A. about 2 pounds

B. about 2 fish

C. about 4 pounds

D. about 5 pounds

(123) Canned and Boxed

Solve.

Find all the ways to put marbles in these cans and boxes to make the total shown. Use the rules below. Show the ways in the table.

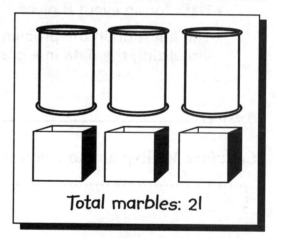

Total marbles: 21

Rules

- Each can must have the same number of marbles.
- Each box must have the same number of marbles.

Marbles in Each Can								
Marbles in Each Box								

⭐**THINK**

Start like this: When there are 0 marbles in each can, is it possible to put marbles in the boxes so the total is 21? Now try 1 marble in each can.

Math Journal Explain how you know you have found all the solutions.

(124) Getting Older

Solve. Explain your work.

The population of Lawton is 38,600. One-fourth of the population is younger than 16, and two-fifths of the population is older than 60. How many people in Lawton are older than 16 but younger than 60?

Answer _____

Math Journal Which age group in Lawton has the greatest number of people: younger than 16, 16 to 60, or older than 60? Explain.

(125) Rainy Day Woes

Solve. Explain your work.

Scott walked home from school in the rain. He left his book bag at school by accident, so his homework got wet. The rain smeared one of his math problems. Scott recopied the problem and wrote boxes for each digit that was smeared. Help Scott fill in the boxes with the correct digits.

$$
\begin{array}{r}
1\ 5 \\
24\overline{)\ \square\,6\,\square\ } \\
-\ \square\square \\
\hline
\square\square\square \\
-\ \square\square\square \\
\hline
0
\end{array}
$$

Answer _____

(126) Fruit Puzzle

Solve. Work backward.

There is a bowl of fruit on the table. There are twice as many apples as there are pears and 1 more orange than there are apples. Eight pieces of fruit are either oranges or bananas. There are 3 bananas. How many pears are in the bowl?

Answer _____

Convince Me Explain how you solved the problem.

Math Journal What was the amount at the end of the problem that you used to solve it? What was the unknown amount at the beginning?

127 Turtle Trucking

Estimate. Use any method you like.
Circle the letter of the correct answer.

A sea turtle rescue organization rescued a 435-lb turtle,
a 175-lb turtle, and a 731-lb turtle. The van the
organization uses to transport turtles to the ocean can
carry 1,500 pounds in the freight area. Can the turtles
all be transported in the van in one trip?

A. No, only two turtles can go together.

B. No, the turtles must weigh 150 pounds more to go in one trip.

C. Yes, all the turtles can be transported in one trip.

D. Yes, but not if the driver weighs a lot.

128 Hop Along

Find the value of each size hop on the number lines below.
Then label the points marked with arrows to show their
value. (*Hint: Hops of the same size have the same value.*)

★**THINK**

Use reasoning to decide
which number line to
solve first.

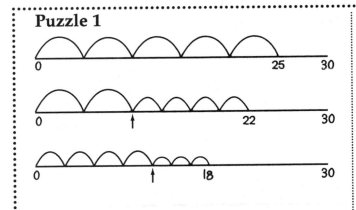

Puzzle 1

Big hop _____

Medium hop _____

Small hop _____

Puzzle 2

Big hop _____

Medium hop _____

Small hop _____

Math Journal Write a number sentence that shows the total value of the
large hops and the medium hops in the second number line in Puzzle 1.

(129) Baaaaaaa

Solve.

TEST TIP
Draw a picture to help you solve the problem.

A rancher had 5,000 sheep. He gave half of them to his daughter. The rancher then gave one-quarter of the sheep he had left to his brother. How many sheep did the rancher keep?

Answer _____

(130) The Coin Game

Solve. Explain your work.

James and Berge are playing a game. They flip three coins at the same time. If the three coins land all heads up or all tails up, James gets 1 point. If the coins land with a combination of heads up and tails up, Berge gets 1 point. Is this a fair game?

Answer _____

Math Journal James suggests they change the rules of the game. They still flip 3 coins, but James gets a point if at least two tails land face up, and Berge gets a point if at least two heads land face up. Is this a fair game? Explain.

(131) Tonnes and Tonnes of Gold

Solve. Write an equation.

The top two gold-producing countries are South Africa and the United States. They produce 915 tonnes (metric tons) of gold each year. South Africa produces 253 tonnes more than the United States. How many tonnes of gold does the United States produce?

Answer _____

Convince Me Explain how you solved the problem.

Math Journal What equation did you used to solve this problem? How can you check your answer?

Estimate. Use any method you like.
Circle the letter of the correct answer.

This summer a blockbuster movie made $16 million the first weekend it opened. The next weekend the movie made 36% less. About how much money did the movie make the second weekend?

A.   about $4,500,000

B.   about $6,000,000

C.   about $10,500,000

D.   about $15,000,000

Math Journal What did you do to the percent in order to solve the problem? Explain.

(133) Hip Hops

Find the value of each size hop on the number lines below. Then label the points marked with arrows to show their value. (*Hint: Hops of the same size have the same value.*)

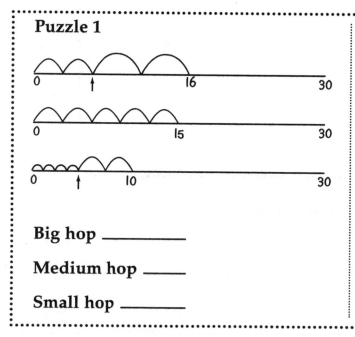

Puzzle 1

Big hop _____

Medium hop _____

Small hop _____

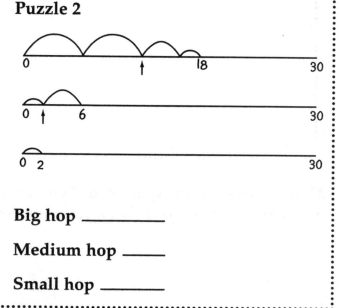

Puzzle 2

Big hop _____

Medium hop _____

Small hop _____

(134) Riding for Dollars

Solve.

Ali rode in a bike-a-thon to raise money for her favorite charity. She had 53 sponsors. Twenty-eight of her sponsors pledged $0.10 for every mile Ali rode. The other sponsors all pledged $0.25 for every mile Ali rode. Ali rode 20 miles in the bike-a-thon. How much money did she raise for the charity?

Answer _____

Math Journal How did you find the number of sponsors who pledged $0.25 per mile? Explain.

(135) An Apple a Day . . .

Solve. Explain your work.

Which is the better price, $2.95 for 2 pounds of apples or $3.95 for 3 pounds of apples?

Answer _____

(136) Jetstream Kelly

Solve. Make a table.

Kelly works in a model airplane factory. She found that 3 planes out of every 28 planes are defective and don't fly straight. If she makes 224 planes, how many planes will not fly straight?

You can **MAKE A TABLE** to solve this problem because

- It has two or more quantities that are related
- Each quantity changes in a pattern

Answer _____

Convince Me Explain how you solved the problem.

Math Journal What number patterns can you find in the table you made?

Newsstand Sales

Solve. Circle the letter of the correct answer.

A magazine company sold 134,289 copies of its January edition.
Each magazine costs $4.25. About how much money did the
magazine company make from selling the January edition?

A. about $520,000

B. about $400,000

C. about $135,000

D. about $40,000

Math Journal What method did you choose to estimate and why?

138 **Hop on Up**

Find the value of each size hop on the number lines below.
Then label the points marked with arrows to show their
value. (*Hint: Hops of the same size have the same value.*)

★**THINK**

Use reasoning to decide
which number line to
solve first.

Puzzle 1

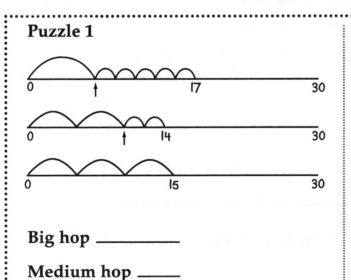

Big hop _____

Medium hop _____

Small hop _____

Puzzle 2

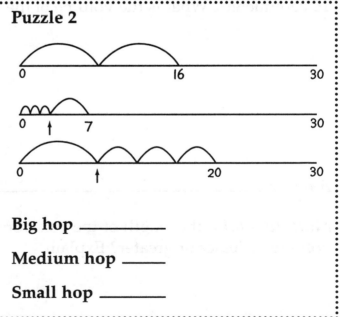

Big hop _____

Medium hop _____

Small hop _____

(139) After-School Shoes

Solve.

There is a law that says any person under 18 years of age may not spend a combined total of more than 48 hours a week in school and at a job. Melody is 16 years old. She goes to school from 7:45 A.M. to 1:15 P.M. each day, Monday through Friday. She also works afternoons at a shoe store. What is the maximum number of hours Melody may legally work each week?

Answer _____

(140) Dimensions of Change

Solve. Explain your work.

Tina keeps her spare coins in a wooden box. The box is a rectangular prism. The length of the box is twice the width. The height of the box is half the width. The length of the box is 16 centimeters. What is the volume of the wooden box?

Answer _____

Math Journal If the length of the box were 12 cm, would the volume be lesser or greater? Explain.

(141) Cleaning Lockers

Solve. Choose a strategy.

Mr. Hines, the principal of Desmond Middle School, likes to give students challenging math problems. He announced that all lockers must be cleaned for a school-wide inspection that would take place in 218 hours, including weekends. The announcement was made at 8 A.M. on Monday. On which day of the week will the locker inspection take place?

Answer _____

Convince Me Explain how you solved the problem.

Math Journal What time of day will the inspection occur? Explain.

(142) Shelving Solutions

Solve. Circle the letter of the correct answer.

A bookstore has a bookshelf that is 413 inches long. The owner of the store wants to put books that are each about 2.54 inches wide on the shelf. About how many books can fit on the shelf?

A. about 100 books

B. about 415 books

C. about 1,000 books

D. about 140 books

(143) Varied Values

Find the value of each size hop on the number lines below. Then label the points marked with arrows to show their value. (*Hint: Hops of the same size have the same value.*)

★**THINK**

Use reasoning to decide which number line to solve first.

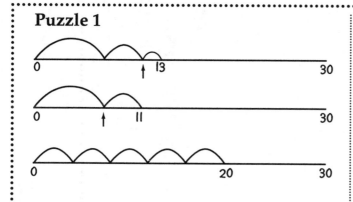

Puzzle 1

Big hop _____

Medium hop _____

Small hop _____

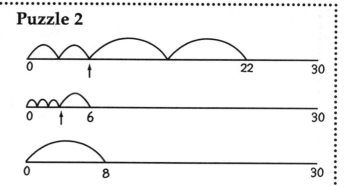

Puzzle 2

Big hop _____

Medium hop _____

Small hop _____

Math Journal Explain how you found the value of the big hop shown in Puzzle 1.

(144) Evening Calls

Solve.

Which telephone company charges less for a
15-minute call between 6 P.M. and 9 P.M.?
How much less?

Company	Time	Cost
Ring My Bell	7 A.M.–5 P.M.	12¢/minute
	5 P.M.–midnight	8¢/minute
	midnight–7 A.M.	8¢/minute
Clear Calls	6 A.M.–midnight	10¢/minute
	midnight–7 A.M.	4¢/minute

Answer _____

_____

(145) Know the Shape

Solve. Explain your work.

Use the given data and what you know about the sides
and angles of different shapes to find the length of each
side and the measure of each angle in each figure.

Square

2 cm

Rectangle

2 cm

5 cm

Parallelogram

120°

2 cm

4 cm

Answer _____

_____

_____

_____

_____

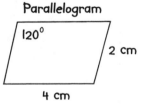

TEST TIP

Write a brief
explanation but
make sure it is
complete.

Math Journal How are the four shapes alike? Explain.

(146) Guests Galore

Solve. Choose a strategy.

The Murphys are having a party. The first time the doorbell
rings, 1 guest enters. The second time the doorbell rings,
3 guests enter. If on each ring a group enters that includes
2 more guests than the previous group, how many guests will
enter on the twentieth ring?

Answer _____

Convince Me Explain how you solved the problem.

Math Journal What strategy or strategies did you use to solve
this problem?

(147) Give Me Pizza!

TEST TIP

Cross out extra information in the problem.

Solve. Circle the letter of the correct answer.

There are 1,180 students at Burnet Hill School. According to a poll, 62% of the students say that pizza is their favorite food to eat for lunch, and 24% of the students say that hot dogs are their favorite food for lunch. About how many students prefer pizza for lunch?

A. about 720 students

B. about 66 students

C. about 1,000 students

D. about 370 students

Math Journal What percent of the students say that neither pizza or hot dogs are their favorite lunch? Explain.

(148) Jumping the Line

★THINK

Use reasoning to decide which number line to solve first.

Find the value of each size hop on the number lines below. Then label the points marked with arrows to show their value. *(Hint: Hops of the same size have the same value.)*

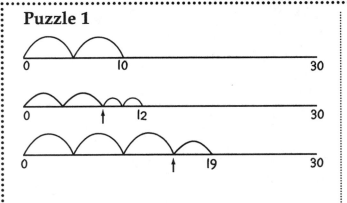

Puzzle 1

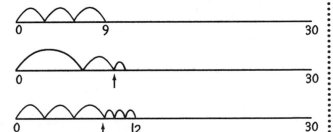

Puzzle 2

Big hop _____

Medium hop _____

Small hop _____

Big hop _____

Medium hop _____

Small hop _____

149 Checks and Bills

Solve.

Kevin gave 10% of his paycheck, or $45, to his mother. Kevin used 12% of his paycheck to pay his phone bill. How much was Kevin's phone bill?

Answer _____

Math Journal In order to solve this problem, did you need to know that 10% of Kevin's paycheck is $45? Explain.

150 Another Number Puzzle

Solve. Explain your work.

Kenny was to assign a number to each student in his class. He could only use the digits 2, 3, and 6 and each person's number had to have 3 digits. Kenny can repeat a digit within a number. Are there enough numbers for all 25 students? Will there be any extra numbers in case new students come into the class?

Answer _____

_____